PENGUIN BOOKS

THE PROMISED LAND

ANDRÉ NAFFIS-SAHELY was born in Venice in 1985 to an Iranian father and an Italian mother, but raised in Abu Dhabi. His poetry has been featured in *Ambit, Areté, The Best British Poetry 2014* (Salt), *New Poetries VI* (Carcanet, 2015), and *Swimmers*, among others. His non-fiction writing has appeared in such publications as *Poetry, The Nation, The Times Literary Supplement, New Statesman* and *The Independent*. He has been awarded fellowships from bodies including the MacDowell Colony and the Dar al-Ma'mûn Foundation. He is also a literary translator from Italian and French; his *Beyond the Barbed Wire: Selected Poems of Abdellatif Laâbi*, winner of a PEN Translates award, was published by Carcanet in 2016.

ANDRÉ NAFFIS-SAHELY

The Promised Land

Poems from Itinerant Life

PENGUIN BOOKS

PENGUIN BOOKS

UK | USA | Canada | Ireland | Australia
India | New Zealand | South Africa

Penguin Books is part of the Penguin Random House group of companies
whose addresses can be found at global.penguinrandomhouse.com

First published 2017
001

Typeset in 10/13.75 pt Warnock Pro by Jouve (UK), Milton Keynes
Printed in Great Britain by Clays Ltd, St Ives plc

A CIP catalogue record for this book is available from the British Library

ISBN: 978–0–141–98493–3

www.greenpenguin.co.uk

Penguin Random House is committed to a
sustainable future for our business, our readers
and our planet. This book is made from Forest
Stewardship Council® certified paper.

for my parents, my brother
and my wife

CONTENTS

I

Petroleum changes human nature.
It ignites people even before it has left the ground.
JOSEPH ROTH

Disposable Cities

They begin as blips on the horizon of prospects, rumours, snippets of exaggerated talk, too fabulous to believe, but too alluring to forget. *Something* has been found: gold, silver, uranium, coltan or oil. Before long, the prospect of immeasurable wealth drowns all incredulity. The migration begins. The engineers in their hard hats and linens are the first on the ground, and with them come derricks, drills, platforms and dry docks. Pipelines sink their tentacles into every lucrative crevice marked on the map. The maps are kept secret.

A handful of shacks are erected to provide a few basic services. Soon enough, the handful swells into a hamlet, then a village, and finally a city. Such cities are the perfect sort of settlement for the modern world: everything is shipped in, everything is easily assembled. Their primary and overriding purpose is to extract, process, and distribute. Just like a motorized pump draws water out of a well, they start inhaling people from all over the world, one desperado at a time.

At first, these fresh arrivals find their new homes unsettling. They find it difficult to adjust to the weird climates and are frazzled by the confusion of languages. No one is under any illusions. They are ephemeral guests, non-citizens; belonging is a dream best forgotten or deferred. Most have come empty-handed, having traded their old lives for grubstakes. Lots of money sloshes around, but most of it is spent simply surviving, and when it runs out, people watch their lives fall apart. Everyone exists in a heightened state of awareness: one false move and they're gone. The poorer they are, the more modest their gambles, which more often than not make them poorer. 'Beggars don't build homelands,' they tell themselves, fantasizing about the day when they might return home and become somebody.

The myth, meanwhile, has travelled to the four corners of the planet. More than cities, these El Dorados are a state of mind, places where people come to reinvent themselves and realize their most eccentric fantasies. All conurbations live out their lot and die, but the disposable cities are special. They thrive in areas of the world generally deemed inhospitable or uninhabitable, in Greenland, Siberia, the Amazon, the Yukon, or the Empty Quarter. They are mushrooms of greed, requiring no loving care or attention, they simply erupt and flourish.

Yet their fame is fleeting. Once bled dry, these cities' roads go raw with potholes, chickens roam loose in the opera houses, power lines sag, and rot seeps in, tarring all in sight. Only those unlucky enough not to make it stay in town for the decline. One day, the wind howls and the last tent comes undone. The lie has moved on to the next disposable city. When I was a child, my mother used to tell me that lies had short legs, and thus could not get very far. Somebody lied to her.

San Zenone degli Ezzelini

There was only a church, a school and a bar
where old men sipped spritzers till dusk.
A dual carriage-way cut through the town,
but nobody ever stopped. Now and then,

there was a car crash; an elderly couple
once burned alive inside their Ferrari
after hitting a lamppost. Their obituary
in the local newspaper read: OUT-OF-TOWNERS,

DEAD. San Zenone was where my father
had taken up carpet-selling: his office
was a storehouse of dust and debts,
with a samovar in view of the window.

The town had once belonged to the Ezzelini,
ruthless warlords who preyed on the weak
in the wastelands between the Pope and the Emperor.
Their most famous son, Ezzelino III, the 'Terrible',

once won his father's soul during a game of dice,
and refused to give it back. In 1254, six years
after he was excommunicated, Pope Innocent IV
yelled '*Let the tyrant die!*' and launched a crusade against him,

the only one ever declared on a single man. It was
the beginning of the end. After months of retreats
and failed sieges, a lone arrow pierced Ezzelino's ankle,
and brought him down at Cassano. Foreseeing

his own doom, Alberico, Ezzelino's brother,
assembled his mercenaries in San Zenone's tower
and waited. From its heights, Alberico watched
as his sons were killed and dismembered,

and his daughters raped and burned. Sometime
before the inevitable, Alberico was told
how Ezzelino's dying breath had betrayed him.
A final act of brotherly love. The tower is featured

on San Zenone's coat of arms, where a giant snake
peers out of the stones, its tongue red and snarling.
'What is that?' I once asked my primary school teacher.
'It reminds us of the poison that lurks in our families.'

Escaping East

It was like going on holiday, permanently.
Even though I was six, I steered my own ship –
or pretended to, perched atop suitcases,
rolling along the corridors at Frankfurt International.

While half the world swept west,
we trickled eastward, one by one,
single-file, like fugitives. Next stop:
Abu Dhabi, where my father had a job

and money, for the first time in years.
Our house was squeezed between
the Russian embassy and a cemetery –
the latter the healthier-looking of the two.

The embassy was a model of the Yeltsin era:
that nauseating smell of rot and booze,
the officers swaying either side of a gate
with a hammer and sickle's silhouette

still legible in the wood. When bored,
I would ring the bell just to hear a drunken 'Da?'
bellow from the other side. The gate stayed shut.
I watched the guards from my mashrabiya,

our first-floor balcony, as they cursed the heat
and loosened their belts. Like them, I put on weight;
everything seemed edible in this city. Everywhere
you looked were fast-food outlets – the vanguard

of globesity. There was so much food, in fact,
that the streets were sticky with its stains and residues.
Each evening, the grocer nearest us left crates
of unwanted mangoes and limes outside his shop;

within hours, they fermented into chutney, leaving
gooey puddles where the cats would feed and fuck.
One day the cemetery gate was left ajar: without
hesitation, I snuck in to breathe some air, a bit of clean air.

Lead, Kindly Light

The school was an hour south of the city, in the middle of nowhere, but the compound was walled and guarded. Our headmaster was a retired policeman, and the windows of the bus were criss-crossed with bars. Submission was the order of the day: you have been given your place in the world, and now you must pay for it. We didn't study much; our books were outdated and censored. As for the rules, they were eminently negotiable. Everyone kept to their own, just like in prison. Suspicions fluctuated with hormones. We knew nothing of the country we lived in, save that our presence was temporary. Our hosts were calm and indifferent. One day, when the subject of oil arose, an Emirati classmate exclaimed: 'My grandfather rode a camel, my father rode a camel, I will drive a Lamborghini, and my son will drive whatever he likes – but my grandson will ride a camel.' The day the USS *Cole* was bombed in Aden, a large Israeli flag was set on fire in the playground. The white kids were nowhere to be seen.

An Island of Strangers

The rooftop was the place to be. I was fifteen
and in love with ash-cans, pigeon coops,
women hanging their laundry. There was a fifty-
foot portrait of the King by the sea,

overlooking a busy junction – always smiling,
like an ad for toothpaste, or mouthwash.
At night, the shore on the west side of town
was the quietest, where hotels, Natashas and *haram*

coalesced into parties. Every half-lit room
was a sure sign of orgasms and the passing
of money from stranger to stranger. Anything
interesting and pleasurable was *haram*. I envied

the King, and his sons, all eighteen of them.
The King was virile, a patriarch, Abraham on Viagra;
his people, on the other hand, were on Prozac.
Everywhere the eye looked was money. The nose

hit only sweat: acrid, pugnacious, pervasive.
Most of the boys I knew sucked Butane, smoked,
saved up for whores, waited for their parole in the summer.
Each back to his own country. Come September

the dissatisfied returned: misfit mutts, at home everywhere
and nowhere. A friend compared cosmopolitanism
to being stuck at summer camp, waiting for parents
who never showed up. In the thirty-third year of his smile,

the King finally died. His mausoleum is a meringue: wavy, white, and empty. His sons have gone on squabbling, playing whose is biggest with bricks. One by one, they die in car crashes. Days of heatstrokes, kif and bloodthirsty Ferraris.

Vanishing Act

Only two out of ten people die in Abu Dhabi; the rest simply fail to have their visas renewed. They are bagged, tagged and placed on the next available flight to wherever they first came from – the one-way ticket experience par excellence. Every edifice on this island is crafted by these almost-nothings. In death, at least, there is solace: never again to queue for days on end, never again to have their fingertips inked and pressed by intolerant hands, their blood screened for undesirable illnesses, their flesh seared by a sun that wonders what the hell they are doing here.

Jumeirah Janes

A hill-station breeze blows through the café:
the ladies are dressed for high tea and the waiters
polish the windows that keep the hot sand at bay.

Life here has left a bitter film on their lips,
which they purse whenever one of them mentions
how her children have gone home and her husband

works six-day weeks even during the summer.
As if that weren't enough, the servants are lazy . . .
Then there are the locals, who are ignorant, venal,

tasteless, and, even worse, lucky. The ladies
are lonely: they want to go back to the You-Kay.
'But then,' one says, 'we're so comfortable here' –

at which point all conspiracy dies. Like
moody nuns, the ladies nod in acknowledgement;
their talk drifts back to the weather.

Mina Zayed

It's late afternoon and the market looks like a used-car lot.
I watch men conduct business from the backs of their trucks;

there's not much on sale today: spices, pots, bags of nuts,
cracked ceramic ashtrays. A few customers stroll by,

but it's too muggy to haggle. The sleepiness of the place
is broken only by the stinging, oddly invigorating smell

of diesel in the air. The port lies just a short distance from here,
and the ships on the horizon rise and dip like the humps

of a great caravan of steel, slowly winding its way
from the West to the Rest. An entire country

is being built from scratch: there are cargo containers
as far as the eye can see. The sun sets, while the market

grows ever more deserted, as if it were the ragged
rear-guard of the past, or an inscrutable prototype of the future.

The Foreign Correspondent

'I do not like the taste in my mouth.
To remonstrate would be better,
to keep my mouth shut would be best.
I can count. I know how many
lost their nerve at the sight of his smile
and how many more died in silence
sliding down the slick wall of his teeth.'

Wanted Man

for my father

For the first time in years, your phone calls stopped.
You were always out of town, or stuck in meetings;
by the time my mother told me, you'd been inside

the best part of a month. One night they came for you
and forty days later, you limped home, your clothes
three sizes too big. Money went missing. While

the thieves took for the hills, you stayed put, oblivious.
By the time the Law figured it out, you'd discovered
how men can be made to fit together like jigsaw pieces

when forty share a room designed for eight.

Months after your release, you wore the confused look
of a character actor left without a part. On the upside,
you 'finally understood the appeal of Johnny Cash.'

Sehnsucht

for my mother

Our family has become a government-in-exile;
visiting you is like paying my respects
to a kindly downhearted minister who
is equally fearful of past, present and future.

Two small rooms to eat and sleep in; only
the essentials escaped being boxed up
while awaiting their destination. Still they wait.
This is home for now – a little town

outside Florence where the streets are lifeless
and the old stick their necks out of windows
like turtles keeping an eye out for vultures.
When apart, we speak only a little:

a pair of talking heads in a penumbra.
I look at you: a housewife without a house,
without a husband too. Pondering it all,
I chew anti-acids with a sovereign indifference.

Your younger son, your adjutant, or aide-de-camp,
shuts himself in his room all day and shoots aliens,
Nazis or terrorists on his console, almost
as if training for a war to reconquer our lives.

Stopover

What city stays still like a glass-cased princess?
I wish this one did. All that hate and here I am.
My whole life, I've hoped to show somebody

this strange town, and now that you're here
I just sit by the creek and mumble something
incoherent in disbelief. Little to do now except

list the sights in a *Guinness Book of Records* way,
or explain how the cafés where I emptied cups
have turned into beauty salons, how the houses

I once lived in are no longer there. Narrow boats
sail past the bright hotels. This whole country
is like a hotel – or a ride in a glass elevator:
sweat, heat; at the ding of the doors, my escape.

The Return

I get stamped in like a tourist. It's seven a.m. and my father's waiting for me at arrivals. We drive along the impossibly wide highways, over the bridge to the island of Abu Dhabi. Sixty years ago, there was almost nothing here: a single mud-brick fort, where the ruler and his family lived, a few brackish wells, an air strip, and a handful of huts. Now it accommodates one and a half million people from just about everywhere on Earth and hosts a Formula 1 Grand Prix. My father pulls up in a parking lot in the middle of Bateen, a residential neighbourhood. On entering the three-storey building where he and my mother live, I spot a succession of bright red crosses spray-painted on nearly every wall, door and hallway. It's Passover at King Herod's. My father explains that an official from the Municipality inspected the building last week and ordered all the partitions torn down in accordance with new planning regulations. Most of the building is held up by light interior walls that sound like ripe watermelons when you rap your knuckles against them. The Municipality has given my parents two days to knock down the walls, or they'll cut off their gas, water and electricity. Over the years, my family has acquired a breath-taking proficiency in paring their lives down to the bare essentials. Living in the United Arab Emirates is like assembling a Jenga tower, then nervously trying to remove as many blocks as you can without the entire edifice collapsing on you. Once the walls are gone, my parents will get a reprieve from the city authorities, like the rest of their anxious fellow tenants: at which point the game starts all over again.

Home After Five Years

My father's head peers over the couch in the dark
and whispers, 'Are you awake?' I don't know,
am I? I'm lying on a mattress on the living room floor,
my hands dank and trembling, wondering if my parents

will survive their mistakes. Nothing like cold sweats
on a warm sulphur Christmas. Outside, the city spills
past the contours of reality. Each time I blink, an island
surges out of the sea: some mad oligarch's wet dream,

or luxury villas for sun-seeking Russian gangsters . . .
At dusk, I stroll along the sliver of beach spared
by the quicksilver illness we call cement.
The boardwalk's semi-deserted, but by the railings,

the lonely Natashas sink their long nails into mangoes
and sigh. 'This is no place to live,' a woman
says to her boyfriend as they puff on their cigarettes:
'Not a place you call home.' I can't argue with that.

All I see are skyscrapers and cranes that raise
even more cranes. As a child, I imagined
those cranes were beanstalks connecting the Earth
to the heavens, but there was no golden goose or giant

in those clouds. Back at the flat, my mother sweeps
gypsum and rubble while crouched on the last
powdery bit of wall that once separated her bedroom
from her kitchen. When we wake up in the morning,

she stares at the sky and looks for rain clouds,
but there's not a single one in sight. The storm

is in her head and her heart. It could be worse;
even flowers still bloom in graveyards . . .

Through the paper-thin wall an inch from my head,
I can hear Hitler ranting and raving to 'Gangnam Style'.
Sharif, our neighbour from Cairo, works at IKEA;
he takes three buses to work and is plagued

by the burdens of bribes, permits and slave wages,
and bears it all with a smile, but why speak of it?
Happiness vanishes the moment it bursts
the levee of the lips; his shivering wife

keeps watch from her balcony like a sailor
forced to weather a storm in a crow's nest.
Starting tomorrow, I'm off again, free as a bird
of passage. Aboard the plane, I'll watch

the island that once looked like my home
continue to grow, swelling like a cancer
on the soft skin of the sea . . . *Come, come, that's
enough now*: remember you chose to live in the fire.

Infidelity

The bin-man lifts the lid
on the hungry, scurvy cats,
and waves a weak hello
as he combs the trash for snacks.

I sit on the balcony semi-naked
and wave back. My cold,
Olympian brutality stirs
with my first cup of coffee

and I catch myself wishing
this town would burn to the ground.
The inexorable sun rises into view
and greases the palms with its light.

A removal van beeps into position.
The piano teacher, my mother's rival,
is preparing herself to move. For months
the two have waged a guerrilla war,

my mother flicking ash into her garden,
the other making clothes slip from their pegs
and mysteriously disappear.
After three years in Florence, my mother

returned to her husband and suddenly
found herself the other woman,
displaced by my father's fear of death –
a male disease that only knows one cure.

Now their conjugal life lies in limbo,
and I watch these people, once jovial,

become slowly infected with nihilism,
hermit crabs too poor for new shells.

But how lasting is love anyway? As Churchill
once said to the King of Bahrain, 'We try
never to desert our friends – that is, unless
it's in our interest . . .' The sun reaches its peak

and a kitten climbs to the top of a small dune
in the half-empty parking lot. It spends an hour
attempting to defecate, but can't: it hasn't eaten enough.
I've seen too much. I shut my eyes and dive back

into the murky ocean of memory.

Flying on New Year's Eve

for my father, again

'Please try to forget us,' my mother said, as I hoisted
myself into the truck with my one good hand.
The other hand was swollen, the size of a dragonfruit:
that was the one I had beaten my brother with.

Our family's falling apart, and he won't even lift
his gaze from the screen. *None of this matters*,
goes his sad generation's motto; 'I'd rather stare at a wall
than read a book,' he told me. All hell broke loose. My

rage wore me like a glove and I landed a right hook
on him, again and again. Later, on the way to the airport,
my father stopped for a pound bag of ice where I buried
my bruised spider. Near the border with Dubai, we passed

a rusty bus crammed with skinny men in blue jumpsuits.
Such men's lives are as cheap as the cloth on their backs,
if not cheaper. Some reward for the follies they build . . .
Now, all along the drive, I try to spot some familiar sight

from my youth, but anything over twenty years old
is a historical landmark, or gone – mostly gone. I could
murder a drink, but that's out of the question . . . Just then,
like a mirage, a round building of the government's,

shaped like a hip-flask, looms from the heat-haze;
the cap won't come undone. When we reach Departures,
almost too late, my father starts to tremble again. It's
his heart-spells: he hasn't eaten anything today and is kept

on his feet by the patriarch's insatiable need to provide,
to appear impervious to ageing. How long will he last?
Old men, unlike old women, seem to wobble into their dotages
like panicky toddlers. I smile like a Sunday drunk and hug

my father goodbye, at which point he says, 'Please
don't forget us.' Then I hear the last call and dash off,
dragging my reluctant ronzinante of a suitcase.
Allah's moral monotony oozes from the loudspeakers.

The Promised Land

Speeding home through a snow-storm,
after a night in the city, my shivering
wife and mother in tow, it occurs to me –
this is not where I should be. Over half

my heart's still buried in sand, the promised
land of oil and honey where father thought
his fortunes would ignite. This night is black,
too black for clarity, and after the autumn's

hunting season, the woods outside the cabin
are devoid of deer. For months I heard
the sound of butchery, heard gunshots mark
each hour's passing while the blurry screen

inside the house related news of death
and misery. Thirty years of sweat and toil
in that curséd desert only for father to hear
a German shout at him: 'Work, nigger, work!'

This is life in Abu Dhabi, a place renowned
for the biggest this and of course the biggest
that. Oh, sure, they got it all: the Louvre,
the Guggenheim, every last accoutrement

of Western snobbery their oil could buy. As for
the biggest heart? After years of exploitation,
of work camps, beatings, and incarcerations,
they tell you, *If you don't like it, leave.* So I left.

Now my father, the old industrious Iranian lion,
his mane reduced to baldness, squats and empties

one bladder of blood after another. It's cold here;
I hate my life; sometimes I also hate my wife;

but mostly I hate this sad, deluded, friendly country:
the USA, with all its lies and all the kids
it shoots in parks and all the men it chokes
to death for selling cigarettes, and all the speeches,

all the acquittals. *Go west, young man, go west*
was sound advice once, but is it any longer? I went
as far west as I could, went south and north
and east only to face the same despair. Dawn breaks,

and while I smoke inside my covered porch I see a deer
press its nose against my window; the trees begin to shake
and soothe me with their music, light slips past the blinds:
even hell is often bright enough to keep some hope alive.

II

It was neither true nor false, it was lived.
ANDRÉ MALRAUX

A Kind of Love

We loved luxury and ate like pigs,
but our room, unborn as yet,
was bare; it was a new building,
and when we moved in, the landlord

looked us over and said, 'No noise
after eleven, please.' Obediently,
for the most part, we adhered,
and kept the ancient record player

(among the only things of mine
to survive the neglect and the moths)
at its lowest; although money
was scarce, vinyl records were cheap

and we took advantage.
Halfway through the tenancy,
I got your name mixed up with
another woman's and, quite rightly,

without a word, you left me there,
taking little else except the needle
you knew full well was irreplaceable,
unlike our short-lived kind of love.

N16 8EA

It's comfortable here. The floors are soft
and up three flights there's a view;
the rent hasn't gone up in years and tomorrow

they're planting trees. If this paradise
were pocket-friendly, I'd take it anywhere . . .
Still, if I keep this patch for some time,

the postman might even learn my name.
How long will my luck hold? If this
were a casino, I would cash my chips in,

but stability, it seems, is a dream that you have
in between one address and another.
This is where my love of roaming led me.

The Translator

for Michael Hofmann

Unshaven and barefoot, as if on a pilgrimage.
His house is blue: the walls, the carpet, the cups;
the kind of blue you see in sad monasteries,

the paint veined and peeling, with brittle bits of gold
hanging on in the rims. Like Gottfried Benn –
a spiritual father figure – he likes to stay home,

where the coffee's better and there's no small-talk.
He seems scattered, has lost a book somewhere:
a translation. All his life he has hidden a language;

now he eats, breathes and interprets it. Later,
our awkwardness spills over Hampstead Heath,
where we walk, mostly in silence. We have soup

and beer around the corner, then take a short-cut
to the bus stop, and he's gone; brought by the wind,
taken back by it: the soft-spoken wunderkind of despair.

Forward March

for my grandfather

You were an odd sight, efficient and pasty-skinned
in the land of perpetual sunbathers. You hated the sea;
love was an unapproachable coastline. Instead,

you preferred mountains, dug-outs, old shells. You had
one overruling obsession, the war: the Second World War,
the one you were too young to fight in. Unfazed,

you brought it home. Your enemies: your Hausfrau
and two daughters. Unlike soldiers, they couldn't surrender.
Films on Rommel, your hero, electrified your frame,

yet despite reading his letters, you overlooked *Krieg
ohne Haß* . . . When senility tried you before its tribunal,
it offered you life (with limitations). You refused.

The Carpet that Wouldn't Fly

for my brother

You sport the sickly ecstasy of the exiles
that people your mother's favourite novels:
quiet, pale-faced, consumptive dreamers.
Your feet, once accustomed to soft sand,
fall heavier now. You lament the peculiar

European fetish for marble, its coldness.
Sometimes at night, in between cigarettes,
you pace the balcony, clap your hands,
as if expecting the cheap rug beneath you
to flout reason and fly you back to the past.

This Most Serene Republic

The marble lions are tarnished and when it rains their once mighty roaring is reduced to a mewl; they're in dire need of a polish, just like the rest of this sad floating republic. My father arrived here in the 1960s, a straniero: *strano e nero*. When the lagoon rose through the fist-sized holes in the floor of his flat, he would huddle atop the immense wardrobes on a mattress and grit his teeth through the winter. Those old, porous palaces, whose upper floors housed the few penniless nobles whose hallowed ancestors once terrorized the Mare Nostrum. Those palaces, much like the one I'm sleeping in, smelt like Latin jungles: mahogany everywhere. I love this tiny room and its Franciscan sparseness. All my life, I've felt like a Jew, or a Gipsy, or some hapless scion of a lost wandering tribe, but they, at least, have Bar Mitzvahs, music . . . all I've left is this room. This was an empire ruled from rooms: chambers decorated for a single, specific purpose: to impress its numerous enemies. I can't sleep. There's a ghostly halo above my bed where a clock used to hang. One way, I suppose, to stake a claim on timelessness, if not serenity.

Venice

Auroville

It was an enlightened apartheid: the spiritually and materially liberated on one side, and we barbarians on the other. Posters along the shaded paths spoke of THE MOTHER'S VISION, but nobody seemed to know what it was. Every other sign read FORBIDDEN. There was a giant golden sphere atop an impossibly manicured lawn: it was a meditation centre, and it too was off-limits. Everything looked shiny and clean, but there was a spiritual sickness in the air. We could see white acolytes prowling around in the distance, their spotless robes gleaming in the sun. All manual labour fell to the lean, chocolate-skinned Tamils; their resentment was palpable. We followed the paths back to the tourist centre and decided on lunch. The visitors' complex looked like a hippie IKEA, and while Aurovillians made no use of paper or coin currencies, we paid for our incense and soap with our dirty rupees. Manufactured to subsidize 'Auroville's plans for a sustainable future', their products are available online, as well as in select upmarket outlets in London, Tokyo, Paris and New York.

Tamil Nadu

Mounting Mileage

I have just arrived in Kolkata after a thirty-six-hour train journey from Chennai: a distance of fifteen hundred kilometres which, according to my ticket, has cost me a rupee per kilometre. I pull out a couple of these coins from my pocket. They're incredibly slim, flimsy almost, like the tinsel-wrapped chocolate doubloons I used to get given at Christmas. Back then, I fantasized I could use them to fund a lavish lifestyle on some tropical island. It wasn't long before I learned that travel required real money, and lots of it. Over time, I have worn countries like shirts or shoes, and shed bits of myself in each. I'm still young, but it already seems obvious that the places I visit and come to love will die before my very eyes, replaced by different versions that, soon, someone younger will come to know and appreciate. This frenetic sort of travelling may simply be my way of 'appeasing the fear of the fugitive', as a German philosopher once put it, but my mounting mileage has only increased my inclination to move; not merely in order to scatter my dust, but because I know that whatever the soul is, travel feeds it.

Kolkata

Feast of the Sacrifice

I watch the King and his courtiers on television as they peg a ram to the floor and slice its throat, then leave the house for a walk. A gluey layer of blood has settled on the cobblestones, and the air smells of scorched fur and lemons. The silence is punctuated by the odd death-bleat in the distance. The medina is entirely deserted: the prayer sounded a while ago and everyone's busy eating. Growing accustomed to the city, I start to fool myself. I'm not a tourist – no: I'm a local; at the very least, a dignified semi-local. An hour into my walk, I notice I'm being followed. I look over my shoulder: there's a boy leaning against a lamppost twenty paces behind me. He couldn't be older than eleven or twelve. He shadows me for a while, then, appearing to lose patience, quickens his pace to catch up to me. His hand clamps my wrist, abnormally strong. 'You're lost,' he tells me; 'you should go home.' Gently, but firmly, as though returning a lost sheep to the fold, he delivers me to my doorstep. He asks for a modest reward. I pay him. He shakes my hand. He has to go: his mother and sisters are waiting for him. At that exact moment, three young men in their twenties appear from around the corner, giggling and singing as they pass a pipe back and forth. The boy eyes them disdainfully. 'They are not men!' he exclaims. Then, pointing a finger at the sky, as though to invoke some higher authority: 'Men must work hard, or stay little forever.'

Fez

Postcard from the Cape

for Declan Ryan and Rachael Allen

Few feet
tread the tired timber floors
of the old Observatory now, a couple
of tourists perhaps, or the odd
data analyst skulking in slippers
down the dark musty corridors.
The security guard is reading *The Pleasure Tube*,
'an exhilarating conspiracy aboard a sexy starship'.

There's no
star-gazing tonight and the clouds
stalk the yellow moon like hungry hyenas.
In 1820, when the Cape had that wet
smell of fever about it, Fearon Fallows
decided his work should devour his life,
and six years after his wife and children had died
he installed his telescope atop Slangkop,

or Snake Hill,
as the Dutch colonists called it.
It's getting late, and the runaways
from the Valkenberg have grown hungry.
Little to eat today, just like yesterday too . . .
A few streets away, the Malay muezzin
clears his throat for the prayer call at the mosque
down in Salt River, past invisible lines

no whites
dare to cross. It's safer indoors,
inside panic mansions with Alsatians

and ARMED RESPONSE signs. David Shook
is in town – one night only! – on his way
to the lush land of Burundi, where the districts
are carved into mountains and the mayors
are 'king of the hill'. He tips an espresso

into a tall Coke –
'Haitian coffee,' he says – and we discuss
how travel can harden the heart, inure it
to pity and pain . . . When dawn breaks,
I go into the garden and watch Devil's Peak
glow like a live coal. My myopia grows worse,
all I see is a blaze – but who needs high definition?
If I close my eyes, the whole world feels like home.

Through the Rockies

It's my third sleepless dawn on the Zephyr
and I'm in Iowa. Outside my window,
a gopher tunnels out of its purgatory
and wobbles across the sugary snow.

Over the aisle, I watch Tanika crush
grains as pink as the sky, then take
a quick hit on her pipe. She's on the run.
Her six kids are somewhere in Indiana;

the last time she spoke to her mother,
the old woman shouted, 'No good
comes of breeding with niggers and spics,'
meaning the fathers of Tanika's children.

'I wish I was in *The Wizard of Oz*,'
Tanika mumbles as we slice
through the American vastness.
Everyone here has one foot in life

and the other in the future, or the past –
usually in the past. Jane, who looks and sounds
like Jessica Lange, reminisces about years
spent working in the circus: 'It was

the '70s. I was living in England,
and you really needed a union card
to get any work as an actress,'
so she spent five gruelling months

touring the continent on an elephant.
Her raw tongue licks the edge

of her jagged teeth: 'The dwarves
were the worst: *mean, horny* things . . .

'One night, two of them tried to rape me,
but the bearded lady, my friend,
gave them a hiding they'll never forget!'
At Reno, Jane and the vets in their caps

begin their week of blackjack and slots.
We slow down before Denver
and during a stop munch our way
through Jane's special brownies;

Lenny, our conductor, plucks a steel guitar
and yells, 'Yo-delay, yo-delay, all aboard!'
Later, he hands me the day's newspaper:
Russia's invaded Crimea again.

If history comes first as tragedy, second as farce,
then what shall we call this third act
we're trying so hard to survive in?
That evening, as we draw near to Chicago,

the passengers turn in unison
to face the horizon; I watch a burst
of dew crystallize in the crisp, purple air,
each droplet shining like a diamond

till it fades away in the distance.
'How pretty,' I think. The next day, Lenny
will tell me this could only mean one thing:
someone was flushing the toilet.

Brief Encounters of the Hopeless Kind

I was running across Chicago's Union Station
and up and down South Canal Street,
looking for a girl with a dog. 'Hey, you!'

a man by his taxi shouted, spotting
the wild look in my eyes. 'You high or what?'
Well, kind of, I thought, but by then

I was clean out of breath and, lacking paper
and pen, or a calm, sober mind, mumbling
a name it was proving too hard to remember.

'Winnie', or 'Whitney,' I'd wanted to say –
'you shake me screw-loose!' But all I had done
at the gate where we parted, after four days

of fast, sleepless travel, was hand her
a card with my name, and an address
no longer my own. She'd set her course:

to hike the frozen spine of the Appalachians.
No dreams of shelters from chaos for her,
just Foxy, her dog, and the open trail . . .

I kept running down the street
till my lungs gave out, nursing the lingering
liquorice of that last, hurried kiss,

and the feel of her tiny frame, and the smell
of her dreads, held in place by a chopstick.
Later, hypnotized by the low flow of the Hudson,

I thought of her as my half-empty Greyhound
rattled through farmlands in New Hampshire,
bought from the Natives, it's said, for a roll of cloth.

Like the granite in the distance, my mind petrified,
while the image of Winnie, or Wendy,
snug in the woods in her sleeping bag,

recalled Francesca's lines to the Florentine:
'*Amor, ch'a nullo amato amar perdona,*'
love will see no reason, love will dig your grave.

Snapping back in my seat, I jumped up
and recalled the train station's refrain:
SEE SOMETHING, SAY SOMETHING. I wished I had.

In the Shadow of Monadnock

for Tomaž Šalamun

The bronze Union soldier
stands guard on the green.
Behind him, the Town Hall

where his forefathers voted
to 'live free or die' is for sale.
The Republic slides to insolvency

and the few YES WE CAN
stickers still in the windows
are beginning to bleach. Spring

loosens its hold on the rivers; the rich
smell of rot wafts out from the leaves.
Something moves in the shadowy pines

that sway in the strong winds and creak
like rusty doors in a horror film.
A fast hammering can be heard:

those woodpeckers know
which tree is next to die. I sit
on the sagging porch of Jo's red colonial

and watch the last ribbons of paint
peel away from the shingles;
there are five bedrooms inside,

but only one is kept warm. No TV
or radio, either: the news upsets Walter.
Jo's girls left long ago, off to plough

the hard field of the City; the milk cow
that saw them to adulthood died last year.
New money is spreading like moss,

while the locals are losing their homes.
'It was easier once: you were born,
you worked the land, and then

the land worked you back into it.'
Now the grocery bags grow thinner
and thinner. Jo means to stick it out.

Birds whose names elude us shatter the silence
in a good way, maybe the best. I inhale the crisp
New England air and exhale a panegyric.

Jo smiles, tells me quite a few folk up here
are suffering from asthma. They can thank
Pennsylvania for that, she says: it's the dust

carried north from the coal mines on the breeze.
'There's hatred, envy and greed afoot in our world,'
wrote an old Saxon poet, 'and this is where you must live:

among thieves and killers.' Back in the square,
I stare into the dead coins of the soldier's eyes
and almost hear the trumpets. There's nowhere to run.

In the Catskills

for Zinzi

We were trapped in a town called Liberty.
Our cabin lay on top of a hill, where the snow
kept us caged for entire weeks at a time.

Down the dirt road, past a couple of bends,
lay the hamlet of Neversink, which of course
had been drowned by a reservoir. It was hard

to think of anything human around us as serious;
all man had built reeked of failure and rust.
We lived amidst the ruined remnants

of a Yankee frontier town – slumbering mills,
silent railroads, idle factories, gutted houses,
a few drowsy strip malls . . . It was the nonsensical

heart of Angry America, where descendants
of Unionists proudly flew Dixie flags
to spite the dark man in the White House.

The one half-decent bite to eat was at Stu's:
a blue Kullman diner formerly on 49th and 11th
that got pushed out by franchises, then

exiled upstate on a flatbed, never to return.
When the mulch plant shut down, the sons
and daughters of Liberty debated at length

the great prospects before them: casinos
or fracking; but the rich second home-owners
fought the oilmen and won, so casinos it was.

'Liberty, son,' an old schoolteacher told me,
'is where the past comes to die.' Ain't it funny to think,
my beloved, that this was where our future began?

III

History is my only country.

ANTAL SZERB

The Other Achilles

'My mother says I have a choice'

The world can do without my name.
Give me a happy backwoods: servants,
a palace, fleets, taxes, maybe a pet too;
a life well lived as any. Pride, I fear,
is pointless. There are no kings, or pawns,
only squares, and a limited number of moves.

Tell me, mother: how long is everlasting?
Not long enough. Let Troy and Greece
fight on without me; no doubt they will. I,
on the other hand, once buried, will fertilize
the green that grows around their ruins, and
like ivy choke their stones, until they crumble:

crumbling, turn to sand.

Atticus

for Mark Ford

                              Unlike many
of the sad schemers Rome birthed in his time,
Titus Pomponius Atticus is best remembered
for how he died, and not for what he tried
and failed to conquer . . .

                              Indeed,
the Gods never abandoned him, as they did
Cicero, Caesar, Brutus and Anthony – yet
to say he played both sides and lived
a long and contented life

                    at the expense of others
would be terribly unjust; in times of need,
friend and foe alike found food and drink
under his canopy, and though he shook
many a hand,

                    none were ever greased.
Seventy-seven and still untouched by scandal,
an ulcer took hold of him, and took him hard.
After three months spent in bed, old Titus,
stoic as ever, placed a hand

                         over his loins
and whispered: 'enough'. That was when
he decided to die, to starve himself
until his life slipped from his lips.
When his fast was in its second day,

                                        the fever,
as though frightened by the man's stubbornness,
left him suddenly. Begged by wife and friends
to relent, Titus submerged himself in silence,
and for three days bore his hunger

                            with the utmost dignity,
until death took him on the fifth. Many wept
at the sight of his litter leaving his home
on its way to the Appian. Little else is known
of Titus, who set still less store by his words,

                              and history,
as if to reward him, has ensured none are remembered –
allowing, by that, no shadow to fall on his memory,
as often befalls a great many of those we hear about,
who gossip without a stray thought for posterity.

Patience

The old Roman emperors knew a thing or two about exile. On discovering a poet who had taken too many liberties, or a relative grown uncomfortably popular, they selected an island, ideally somewhere sunny: Africa, perhaps, or a rocky outpost off the coast of Sicily; then, having chosen a location that was suitably isolated, they dispatched their prisoner there. At first, life wasn't so bad for the new exile. Letters from friends came and went, and slaves catered to their every need. The climate was pleasant; the villa spacious; their allowance ample; and their stay, they were assured, only temporary. The exile was allowed to roam freely within the village. Occasionally, they even made friends. As the years went by, a routine of small pleasures would help to mitigate the exile's nostalgia, making their longing almost bearable. Languishing in indolence, however, the exile would grow to look upon his changeless fate as worse than death itself. Finally, when the Emperor saw that sufficient time had elapsed, the soldiers were dispatched: small handfuls of men-at-arms who, washing ashore on the island under cover of darkness, would bring the long vacation to its promised end.

The Crisis of the Third Century

They were dying, the Romans, and they knew it:
fewer sandals took to their roads, and wars
were getting pricier, bloodier; less satisfying, too.

Once fear got hold of the Romans,
it never released them. Their solution was walls,
higher walls: the blind ecstasy of mortar and brick.

The more spirited ones threw lavish parties,
orgies – their spirits sinking as each of their guests
abandoned sinful pleasures for the sanctity of the Cross.

Some blamed it all on the polluting barbarians,
and edicts were passed to outlaw the mixing of races.
Of all their flawed remedies, it would be their last.

The Pagan's Lament

'The Christians burned down my father's school
and across the sea, by the mouth of the Nile,
they butchered a colleague of his in her classroom.
I'm told she was beautiful: curly locks, full lips
and a mind as bodacious. Unlike my old father,
I keep my opinions to myself; my husband
fervently believes in a God who some
describe as jealous, a murderer, even. My husband's
friends frighten me: last night they slaughtered
a man for insisting an angel might also
be called a nymph – one of the finer points
of their canonical law . . . Today I heard my husband
say a rational woman was a sign of decadence,
of end times. I see dark days ahead for my kind.'

Put Not Your Trust in Princes

After four decades of early mornings and late nights,
Ferdowsi had completed his epic, the *Shahnameh*,
and thus he decided to visit Sultan Mahmoud,
who'd once promised him a gold piece per couplet;

Ferdowsi had written sixty thousand of them . . .
Unfortunately, Sultan Mahmoud was dejected:
the long years of peace were proving hard to bear
without the rich, gluey feel of blood on his hands.

He sent the poet home with a mere sack of silver.
Years later, as the Sultan was about to ride into battle,
a minister recited a sad song of singular beauty.
When the Sultan learned Ferdowsi was its author,

he immediately sent him a caravan laden with gold;
but as the caravan entered the city through one gate,
Ferdowsi's remains were being wheeled out the other.

ACKNOWLEDGEMENTS

Thanks are due to Donald Futers at Penguin for guiding this book to life. I am also grateful to Jin Auh and Alba Ziegler-Bailey at the Wylie Agency for their support. I would like to extend my gratitude to the editors of the following publications, where some of the poems in this book first appeared: *Ambit, Areté, Night & Day, PN Review, Poetry London, Swimmers, The Warwick Review, The Yellow Nib* and *World Literature Today*. Thanks are also due to the editors of the following anthologies: *New Poetries VI* (Carcanet, 2015), *The Best British Poetry 2014* (Salt), *Oxford Poets Anthology 2013* (Carcanet) and *Days of Roses II* (2012). 'The Other Achilles' was awarded the G. S. Fraser Poetry Prize in 2010. I am grateful to the MacDowell Colony, where I assembled this manuscript in spring 2014. I am indebted to David Harsent and Declan Ryan for their kindness and unwavering support. This book also owes its existence to my teachers and mentors, both formal and informal: Nick Everett, Don Paterson, Sarah Maguire, Mark Ford and Jamie McKendrick. Special thanks to Aamer Hussein, Michael Schmidt, Robert Selby and Malene Engelund.